Explore Satellites

Lola Schaefer

Lerner Publications ◆ Minneapolis

Lerner Publications Company
An imprint of Lerner Publishing Group, Inc.
241 First Avenue North
Minneapolis, MN 55401 USA

For reading levels and more information, look up this title at www.lernerbooks.com.

Main body text set in Billy Infant Regular. Typeface provided by SparkType.

Library of Congress Cataloging-in-Publication Data

Names: Schaefer, Lola M., 1950- author.
Title: Explore satellites / Lola Schaefer.
Description: Minneapolis, MN: Lerner Publications Company, an imprint of Lerner Publishing Group, Inc., [2023] | Series: Lightning bolt books. Exploring space | Includes bibliographical references and index. | Audience: Ages 6-9. | Audience: Grades 2-3. | Summary: "How can you watch your favorite TV shows almost anywhere? How do scientists learn what's happening in far off galaxies? Readers discover how satellites make our lives easier and keep people safe . . . all from space!"—Provided by publisher.
Identifiers: LCCN 2021043419 (print) | LCCN 2021043420 (ebook) | ISBN 9781728457802 (lib. bdg.) | ISBN 9781728463476 (pbk.) | ISBN 9781728461588 (eb pdf)
Subjects: LCSH: Artificial satellites—Juvenile literature.
Classification: LCC TL796.3 .S33 2023 (print) | LCC TL796.3 (ebook) | DDC 629.46—dc23/eng/20211028

LC record available at https://lccn.loc.gov/2021043419
LC ebook record available at https://lccn.loc.gov/2021043420

Manufactured in the United States of America
1-50808-50147-2/11/2022

Table of Contents

Signals from Space

A sports fan turns on a TV. It sends a signal to the satellite dish on the roof. The dish sends the signal to a TV satellite in space.

The TV satellite responds. It sends information to the sports fan's satellite dish and TV. The sports fan watches a soccer game.

Satellites send us signals that let us watch programs such as sports games.

The Story of Satellites

The moon is a natural satellite that spins around Earth. The moon orbits the planet.

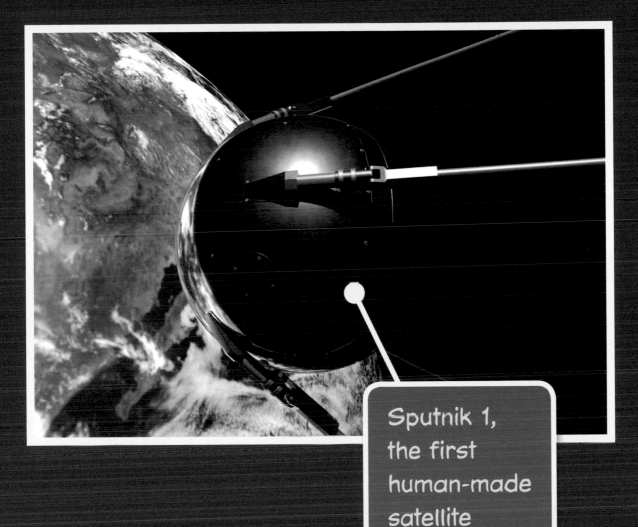

Sputnik 1, the first human-made satellite

The first satellite made by humans took its first trip around Earth in 1957. Each orbit took about ninety-eight minutes.

Scientists use satellites to monitor weather, oceans, and gases in our air. Satellite data helps keep us safe.

Scientists get weather information from satellites using satellite dishes.

Satellites can track forest fires and smoke. They even let us know when rocky space objects come close to Earth.

Satellites help firefighters find and stop forest fires.

Many satellites send information to GPS devices. They tell us where we are and how to go somewhere else.

Information from GPS satellites helps us explore the world.

Some satellites take pictures of galaxies more than two million light-years away.

Other satellites send us data about our sun and moon. Some send data about other planets and faraway stars.

Satellites in Action

Satellites ride rockets into space. Large solar cells on a satellite's wings change sunlight into power.

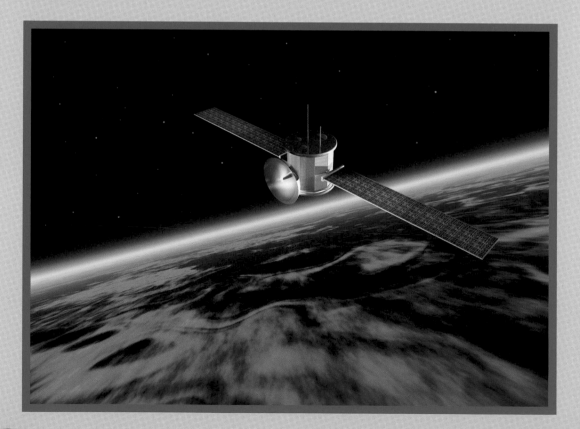

Every satellite holds
computers and thrusters.
Thrusters keep the satellite
from falling down to Earth.

Satellites often carry a payload. Devices like cameras, telescopes, and sensors make up payloads.

The Hubble Space Telescope carries mirrors that help us see far away in space.

A satellite's transponder receives signals from Earth. It sends signals out to satellite dishes and sensors on other machines.

Into the Unknown

Space stations are satellites where people live and work. Scientists are planning to build larger space stations.

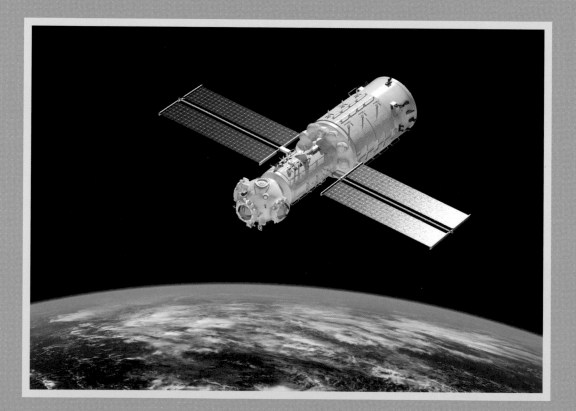

Some space stations will be science labs. Others might be hotels for space travelers.

Scientists on the International Space Station study space and Earth.

The Mars Reconnaissance Orbiter was launched in 2005. It orbits Mars and takes close-up photos of the planet.

Satellites explore Mars and other planets. In the future, satellites might even explore planets orbiting other stars.

We have so much more to learn about Earth and space. Will you help make a satellite one day?

Satellite Diagram

transponder

platform (body)

antenna

wings with
solar cells

thrusters

Watching the Oceans

On November 21, 2020, the Copernicus Sentinel-6 satellite sailed into space on a rocket. For five and a half years, it will monitor the oceans with the Jason-3 satellite. The satellites measure the rise of sea levels and help predict flooding. They send this information to scientists on Earth. The data shows scientists how climate change affects the oceans. This information can save the lives of people who live near the sea.

Glossary

data: information or facts

GPS: a system that uses signals from satellites to find the user's location and give directions to other places

monitor: to watch or check something

orbit: to travel around a planet, moon, or other object in space

payload: devices that a satellite carries such as antennas, cameras, telescopes, space probes, and sensors

sensor: a device that can detect changes in heat, motion, and sound

thruster: a small rocket engine on a spacecraft used to change direction or height

transponder: a device for sending and receiving radio signals

Learn More

NASA: Build Your Own Spacecraft!
https://spaceplace.nasa.gov/build-a-spacecraft
/en/

NASA Science Space Place: How Does GPS Work?
https://spaceplace.nasa.gov/gps/en/

NASA Science Space Place: Where Do Old Satellites
Go When They Die?
https://spaceplace.nasa.gov/spacecraft
-graveyard/en/

Schaefer, Lola. *Explore Rockets.* Minneapolis: Lerner
Publications, 2023.

Sparrow, Giles. *Space Travel.* New York: Enslow,
2018.

Woolf, Alex. *The Science of Spacecraft: The Cosmic
Truth about Rockets, Satellites, and Probes.* New
York: Franklin Watts, 2019.

Index

Photo Acknowledgments

Image credits: Amirul Syaidi/EyeEm/Getty Images, p. 4; Jose Luis Pelaez Inc/Getty Images, p. 5; Kevin Gill/Wikimedia Commons CC BY-SA 2.0, p. 6; Rodichev Vitalii/Shutterstock.com, p. 7; Ryan McGinnis/Getty Images, p. 8; Ruslan Lusi/EyeEm/Getty Images, p. 9; SrdjanPav/Getty Images, p. 10; NASA/Swift/Stefan Immler (GSFC) and Erin Grand (UMCP), p. 11; artpartner-images/Getty Images, p. 12; NASA, p. 13; jamesbenet/Getty Images, p. 14; sdecoret/Shutterstock.com, p. 15; xia yuan/Getty Images, p. 16, 20; NASA/JSC, p. 17; Science Photo Library/Alamy Stock Photo, p. 18; Slingshot/Getty Images p. 19.

Cover: 3DSculptor/Getty Images.